TopReaders

Traders and Travelers

Robert Coupe

Contents

Early Civilizations 4

Traders at Ostia 6

Desert Traders 8

European Trade 10

Sailing West 12

Trade by Canal 14

An Ancient Capital 16

Passage to India 18

Sir Francis Drake 20

Exploring Africa 22

Russian Trade 24

Trade with Japan 26

Canals 28

Quiz 30

Glossary 31

Index 32

n earlier times, people made long, dangerous journeys
o trade their goods and explore distant countries.
We can now travel great distances in a very short time.
Modern transport is speedy and safer than in the past.

Early Civilizations

Five thousand years ago, ancient Egypt and Sumer were great civilizations. People there grew crops and raised animals. They made long journeys to trade goods with each other. They were the first people to keep written records of the things they traded.

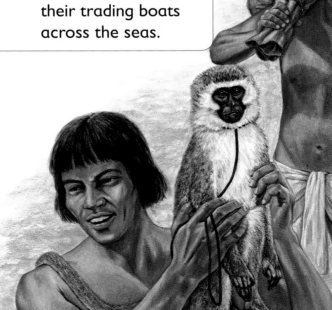

Egyptian Trading Boat

By about 5,000 years ago, Egyptians had invented sails. Before that, they used oars to pull their trading boats across the seas.

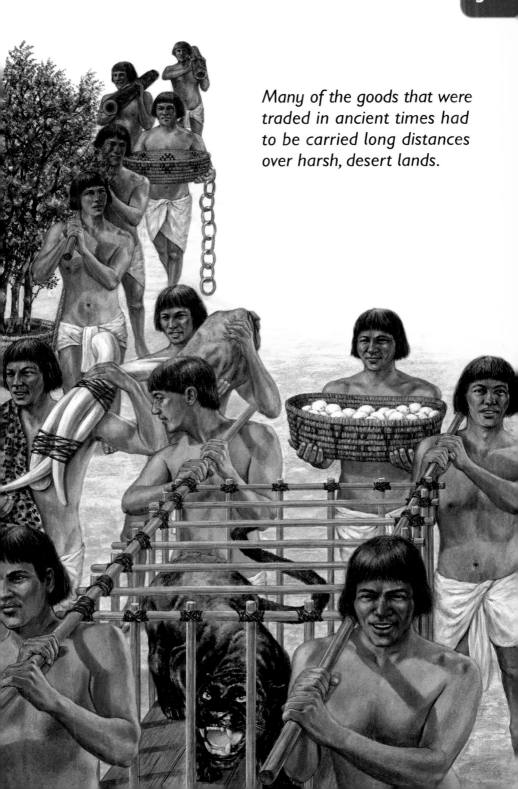

Many of the goods that were traded in ancient times had to be carried long distances over harsh, desert lands.

Wine, and oil for lamps and cooking, were brought to ancient Rome in tall red pottery jars called amphorae *.*

Fact File

Gladiators in ancient Rome fought against wild animals. Thousands of people came to watch these fights. Tigers from Asia, rhinoceroses from Africa, and bears from Scotland were brought to Rome for the contests.

Traders at Ostia

Ostia is a seaport near Rome. In ancient times, sailboats brought goods from faraway places into this port. Rowboats then took these goods along the River Tiber into the city of Rome. The sailboats were too large to travel along the shallow river.

Desert Traders

The Sahara Desert is in northern Africa.
Over many centuries, traders used camels
to carry goods across this harsh, dry region.
These traders came from countries near and far,
and stopped at oases to collect food and water.

Traders in Africa often captured people and made them into slaves .

European Trade

The period in history between about 1,500 and 550 years ago is called the Middle Ages. During this time, trade between Europe and other parts of the world grew rapidly. Merchants sent goods to be sold in distant places. Many merchants became very rich people.

The Black Death

A terrible plague spread through Europe during the 1300s. People called it the Black Death. It killed about 25 million people.

People begin to load goods beneath the deck of a trading boat in Hamburg, Germany, during the 1300s.

Sailing West

In 1492, Christopher Columbus set sail from Spain. He commanded a fleet of three ships. They sailed west across the Atlantic Ocean. Eventually, they reached some islands. Columbus thought they were in Asia and he named these islands the West Indies.

Shipwreck!

The *Santa Maria* was the ship in which Columbus sailed from Spain. It was wrecked in the Caribbean and did not return to Spain.

After two months at sea, there was great excitement when a sailor saw land. The fleet of ships had reached the Caribbean Sea. They were close to the coast of America.

Trade by Canal

China is an ancient country. More than 2,000 years ago Chinese people built canals . These canals stretched between rivers. They created waterways between cities. Along the canals, boats carried food and other goods for trade over long distances.

Some people in ancient China lived on the boats that sailed along canals.

Early Compasses

Many inventions came from ancient China. This compass has a magnetized needle floating in a bowl of water. It helped sailors to find their way safely over vast oceans.

An Ancient Capital

For many centuries, the city of Chang'an was the capital of ancient China. About 1,200 years ago, two million people lived there. Many of them were rich. Traders from many parts of Asia brought goods to sell in the busy markets of Chang'an.

Preparing Pots

Colorful pots like this one were sold in Chinese markets. Artists painted pots and other objects with colored sap from lacquer trees.

People could buy all kinds of products in Chang'an's markets. Acrobats and musicians entertained the shoppers.

Passage to India

During the 1400s, sailors from Portugal began traveling southward. They sailed in small ships called caravels. They gradually moved farther south along the west coast of Africa. In 1498, the explorer Vasco da Gama sailed around Africa and finally landed in India.

The people in some parts of Africa welcomed the Portuguese sailors. In other places, they were hostile.

The Spice Trade

Spices such as mace and nutmeg were used in past times to hide the taste of old meat. European traders brought back spices from India and other parts of Asia.

Sir Francis Drake

Sir Francis Drake was the most famous English sailor of the 1500s. In 1577, he sailed his ship, the *Golden Hind* southward from England. He returned three years later. He had sailed right around the world. On his journey, he attacked many Spanish ships and stole their cargoes.

During his voyages, Drake collected gifts for the English queen, Elizabeth I. Here he presents her with a stolen pearl necklace.

☆ Fact File

In **1588**, the king of Spain was so angry with Drake that he sent a fleet of ships to try to invade England.

The Slave Trade

For more than 300 years, African people were captured and sold as slaves. During long voyages across oceans, they were kept in chains. Many slaves died along the way.

Exploring Africa

People from many countries set up trading ports in Africa. They hunted elephants for their ivory tusks. They dug into the earth to mine diamonds. They captured Africans and made them slaves. They sent these slaves to India, the Middle East, and America.

These miners in Africa are tunneling through rock to find gold. Later, gold in Africa was mined deep below ground.

Russian Trade

In 1728, a Danish explorer, Vitus Bering, discovered a sea route between Russia and Alaska. This route is called the Northeast Passage. Russian hunters sailed to Alaska to hunt fur seals, sea otters, and walruses. These animals have thick, warm fur.

Russian hunters also trapped land animals for their fur.
These trappers are selling Arctic fox furs to English traders.

Trade with Japan

Until the 1800s, there was little trade between Japan and other countries. In 1854, four American warships sailed into Edo Bay, in Japan. This is now called Tokyo Bay. A year later, the United States and Japan signed a treaty . They agreed to trade with each other.

Fact File

After 1854, many people in Japan, including the Royal Family, began wearing clothes like those worn in Europe and America. For them, this was the modern way to dress.

Soon after the Americans sailed into Edo Bay, ships from Britain and France arrived in Japan.

Canals

The Suez Canal, in Egypt, joins the Mediterranean and the Red seas. It opened in 1869. It made the sea journey between Europe and Asia much shorter. In 1914, the Panama Canal, in Central America, was completed. It joins the Pacific and Atlantic oceans.

Getting Wider

The Suez Canal has been made wider and deeper twice.
This allowed bigger and bigger ships to sail through it.

1869   1939   today

*Crowds gathered
to watch the first
ships steam along the
Suez Canal in 1869.*

Quiz

Can you unscramble the words and match them with the right pictures?

SHICAN

MASLEC

SCAPSOM

LEVARCAS

Glossary

amphorae: large jars with narrow necks that were used in ancient Rome for storing wine, olive oil, and fish sauce

canals: waterways that people make by digging out the land between rivers or seas

caravels: small sailing ships with two or three masts

gladiators: people in ancient Rome who were trained to fight against other gladiators or against wild animals

magnetized: like a magnet, being able to pull other objects toward it or to be pulled toward other objects

merchants: people who buy and sell goods in order to make a profit

Middle East: the part of the world around the southern and eastern shores of the Mediterranean Sea

plague: a terrible disease that spreads quickly through a country or over a large area

slaves: people who belong to other people and are forced to work for them

Sumer: an ancient country in part of what is now Iraq

trade: the buying and selling of goods between different regions or countries

treaty: an agreement between different countries. In treaties, countries can agree to trade with or not attack each other.

waterways: bodies of water that lead between places

Index

Africa	6, 8, 9, 18, 22, 23
Black Death	10
camels	8, 9
Chang'an	16, 17
China	14, 15, 16
Columbus, Christopher	12
Drake, Sir Francis	20
Egypt	4, 28
Europe	10, 26, 28
India	18, 19, 22
Japan	26
Ostia	6
Panama Canal	28
Portugal	18
Russia	24
slaves	9, 22
Spain	12, 20
Suez Canal	28, 29
Sumer	4
West Indies	12